GET INFORMED—STAY INFORMED

IMMIGRATION AND REFUGEES

Heather C. Hudak

CRABTREE

PUBLISHING COMPANY
WWW.CRABTREEBOOKS.COM

Author: Heather C. Hudak
Series Research and Development:
Reagan Miller
Editor-in-Chief: Lionel Bender
Editor: Ellen Rodger
Proofreaders: Laura Booth,
Melissa Boyce
Project coordinator: Petrice Custance
Design and photo research:
Ben White
Production: Kim Richardson
Production coordinator and
prepress technician: Tammy McGarr
Print coordinator: Katherine Berti
Consultant: Emily Drew,
The New York Public Library

Produced for Crabtree
Publishing Company by
Bender Richardson White

Photographs and reproductions: Alamy: 28 (Kathy deWitt),
29 (Jim West), 33 (Richard Levine), 35 (Zoonar GmbH); Firefly
Books: 13 (cover illustration Jackie Roche); Getty Images: 4–5
(Pedro Pardo), 25 (Robert Nickelsberg), 26–27 (Yasin Ozturk/
Anadolu Agency), 30–31 (Geoff Robins/AFP), 36–37 (John
Moore), 38–39 (Christian Ender), 40–41 (Louisa Gouliamaki);
Library of Congress: 17; Shutterstock: 1 (Sk Hasan Ali), 1
(Julien_N), 6 (joyfull), 6–7 (Anjo Kan), 8–9 (hikrcn), 10–11
(Stacey Newman), 12 (fizkes), 14–15 (Janossy Gergely), 15
(Alessandro Pietri), 22 (Everett Historical), 24 (Christopher
Penler), 32 (Frederic Legrand – COMEO), 34–35 (AAraujo),
36 (arindambanerjee), 39 (Sk Hasan Ali), 43 (Sherry V Smith),
42–43 (Jacob Lund); Topfoto: 16, 20–21 (Heritage–Images), 17,
18, 19 (Granger, NYC), 20 (IMAGNO/
Austrian Archives (S));
Icons & heading band: shutterstock.com

Diagrams: Stefan Chabluk, using the following as sources of
data:
p. 7 U.S. Homeland Security and Government of Canada
immigrations figures
p. 11 United Nations Refugee Agency
p. 23 U. S. Holocaust Memorial Museum
p. 30 U.S. Homeland Security
p. 32 U.S. National Bureau of Economic Research
p. 35 Gallup/Statista.com
p. 39 U.S. Homeland Security

Library and Archives Canada Cataloguing in Publication

Title: Immigration and refugees / Heather C. Hudak.
Names: Hudak, Heather C., 1975- author.
Description: Series statement: Get informed, stay informed |
Includes bibliographical references and index.
Identifiers: Canadiana (print) 20189056509 |
Canadiana (ebook) 20189056517 |
ISBN 9780778753339 (hardcover) |
ISBN 9780778753476 (softcover) |
ISBN 9781427121943 (HTML)
Subjects: LCSH: Emigration and immigration—Juvenile literature.
| LCSH: Immigrants—Juvenile literature. | LCSH: Refugees—
Juvenile literature.
Classification: LCC JV6035 H83 2019 | DDC j304.8—dc23

Library of Congress Cataloging-in-Publication Data

CIP available at the Library of Congress

Crabtree Publishing Company

www.crabtreebooks.com   1-800-387-7650

Printed in the U.S.A./032019/CG20190118

Published in Canada
Crabtree Publishing
616 Welland Ave.
St. Catharines, ON
L2M 5V6

Published in the United States
Crabtree Publishing
PMB 59051
350 Fifth Avenue, 59th Floor
New York, NY 10118

Published in the United Kingdom
Crabtree Publishing
Maritime House
Basin Road North, Hove
BN41 1WR

Published in Australia
Crabtree Publishing
Unit 3 – 5 Currumbin Court
Capalaba
QLD 4157

CONTENTS

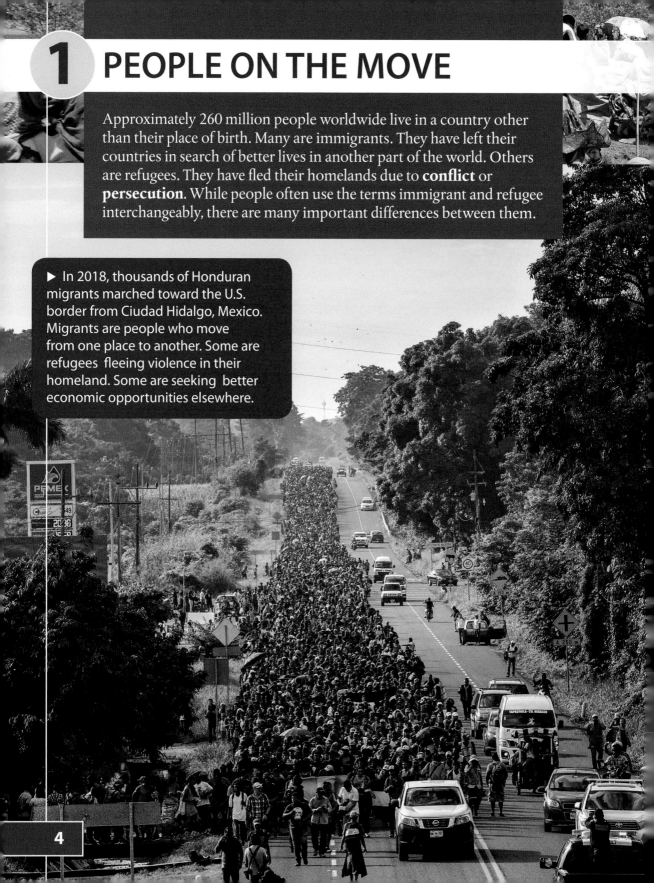

PEOPLE ON THE MOVE

Approximately 260 million people worldwide live in a country other than their place of birth. Many are immigrants. They have left their countries in search of better lives in another part of the world. Others are refugees. They have fled their homelands due to **conflict** or **persecution**. While people often use the terms immigrant and refugee interchangeably, there are many important differences between them.

▶ In 2018, thousands of Honduran migrants marched toward the U.S. border from Ciudad Hidalgo, Mexico. Migrants are people who move from one place to another. Some are refugees fleeing violence in their homeland. Some are seeking better economic opportunities elsewhere.

QUESTIONS TO ASK

Within this book are three types of boxes with questions to help your critical thinking about immigration and refugees. The icons will help you identify them.

THE CENTRAL ISSUES
Learning about the main points of information.

WHAT'S AT STAKE
Helping you determine how the issue will affect you.

ASK YOUR OWN QUESTIONS
Prompts to address gaps in your understanding.

REASONS FOR LEAVING

Immigrants are people who choose to leave their homeland. They hope to find more job opportunities, a better way of life, more freedom to follow their beliefs, and/or be reunited with family members who left previously. They leave their countries willingly. If they so choose, most immigrants can return to their homelands whenever they want.

Refugees, on the other hand, usually have no choice but to leave their homelands. They come from countries that are being ripped apart by war, famine, **natural disasters**, or violent gangs. Many refugees fear persecution in their homelands because of their race, culture, or beliefs. They do not necessarily want to leave, but they are forced to do so. Refugees cannot safely return to their homelands unless the conditions in that country change, which does not happen very often.

A GROWING PROBLEM

Globally, there are about 50 percent more people living in places other than their homelands than there were in the year 2000. About one out of every 113 people is a refugee, and every three seconds someone, somewhere, is displaced from their home due to conflict or persecution. As these numbers continue to rise, it is important to understand the challenges refugees and immigrants face as they try to rebuild their lives in new countries.

> *To those fleeing persecution, terror and war, Canadians will welcome you, regardless of your faith. Diversity is our strength.*
>
> Canadian Prime Minister Justin Trudeau

5

The topic of immigration and refugees is of great importance around the world. From understanding the reasons why some people leave their homelands to the restrictions some **host countries** make on the numbers of them they allow to enter each year, this is an issue that impacts everyone.

In recent years, there have been several events that have brought the topic of immigration and refugees into the spotlight. One of the most significant began in 2011 when a **civil war** broke out in Syria that forced millions of people to flee. Hundreds of thousands of people have been killed in the fighting and more than 13 million are in need of help. Newspapers and TV shows documented their plight as they escaped the dangers in their homeland.

TOLERANCE AND UNDERSTANDING

Getting informed and understanding the reasons why people leave their homes helps foster **tolerance** and acceptance rather than fear and persecution. When people are misinformed they can jump to wrong conclusions. This may lead to unfair treatment, such as prejudice or **discrimination**, toward newcomers into a host country. In some cases, people become **complacent**, believing there is nothing they can do to change the situation both in other parts of the world and in their own communities.

Being informed helps you understand the world around you and how global events impact your own life. It also helps create a well-balanced point of view so you can make informed decisions of your own. Once you get informed about the issues, it is important to stay informed with the most current details as facts and theories change over time.

THE CENTRAL ISSUES

Why do you think there are so many more migrants today than in the past? What current events around the world might be causing refugees to flee? How might the mass migration of people have an impact on **society**, and what strategies do you think goverments need to put in place to deal with it?

▶ In 2018, more than 100,000 refugees arrived by sea in Greece, Italy, Spain, and Cyprus. Many were from Syria and Afghanistan and they sailed on overcrowded dinghies from Turkey. In Greece, more than 200 refugees registered each day.

" *Refugees are not terrorists. They are often the first victims of terrorism.* "

António Manuel de Oliveira Guterres, former United Nations (UN) High Commissioner for Refugees

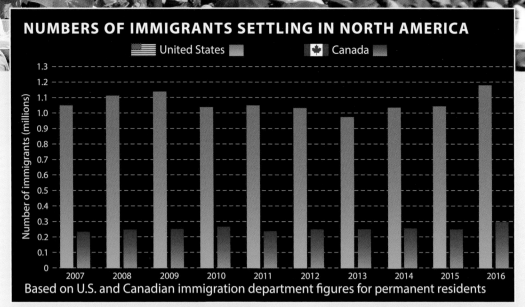

NUMBERS OF IMMIGRANTS SETTLING IN NORTH AMERICA

United States ▬ | Canada ▬

Y-axis: Number of immigrants (millions) — 0, 0.1, 0.2, 0.3, 0.4, 0.5, 0.6, 0.7, 0.8, 0.9, 1.0, 1.1, 1.2, 1.3

X-axis: 2007, 2008, 2009, 2010, 2011, 2012, 2013, 2014, 2015, 2016

Based on U.S. and Canadian immigration department figures for permanent residents

ARRIVAL IMMIGRATION

◄ Arrivals at Changi Airport, Singapore. Singapore does not take part in international refugee protection programs or have any national refugee policies. As a result, most refugees are likely to be **detained** or **deported**.

2 HOW TO GET INFORMED

With any topic, first consider its context. This refers to its background or setting. Context helps identify the key issues and creates a connection between you and the world around you. It will give you the information you need to better understand the topic. In order to build context, you need to gain a complete overview of the topic. This involves learning about the topic's history, key people, important events, and the current state of affairs. To get this in-depth knowledge, you need to refer to **source materials**.

▶ Dadaab refugee camp in Kenya is one of the largest in the world. Established in 1991, it is the temporary home of more than 235,000 registered refugees and asylum seekers.

KEY INFORMATION

Migrant refers to anyone who moves away from their homeland.

Homeland is the country where a person was born or has spent most of their life.

A **host country** is a country that takes in and looks after an immigrant or refugee.

Asylum seekers are people whose claim for refugee status in a host country has not yet been approved.

Alien is a negative term for an undocumented immigrant, or a person who lives in a country without its authorization.

Illegal immigrants are people who enter a country without a **visa** or who remain in a country after their visa expires.

Internally displaced persons (IDPs) are people who are forced to leave their homes but remain in their homeland.

Registered refugees are people who have gone through a legal process to gain refugee status in a host country.

GETTING STARTED

There are two main types of source materials: primary and secondary. Primary sources are created by people who have firsthand experience of the subject matter. For immigration and refugees, they may be people who have **emigrated** from another country, worked for an organization providing support for refugees, or helped welcome a newcomer into a host country. Examples include:

- autobiographies written by immigrants or refugees about their life and experiences migrating to a new place
- survey results outlining how people feel about bringing immigrants or refugees into their country
- photographs of refugee camps or of refugees in overcrowded boats
- recordings of radio interviews with recent immigrants talking about why they chose to relocate
- streaming **media** sites showing conflict in a war-torn nation or people waiting in line to register as refugees.

Secondary sources of information are created after the events and often far from the action. Secondary sources are made by **analyzing** and **interpreting** other primary and secondary sources. Examples of secondary sources include:

- a Hollywood movie about people who came to North America in the 1800s to settle the land and escape persecution in Europe
- books written by historians summarizing the experiences of immigrants and refugees
- blog posts based on past immigration events.

SOURCES OF INFORMATION

From blogs and podcasts to magazines and encyclopedias, it is easy to find a wealth of information on almost any subject. In fact, there is sometimes so much information to sort through that researching a new subject can be a daunting task. Knowing where to start can be intimidating, but there are some research tools you can use to make it easier.

WHERE TO LOOK

Start at a library. Libraries have a wide range of both fiction and nonfiction books plus reference materials, historic documents, DVDs, music, magazines, and more. Ask a librarian for assistance to help you locate the information you seek. The Internet is another powerful research tool. Public records, such as **statistics** and government papers, are often posted online. There are also many digital newspapers, magazines, and journals. Other items available on the Internet include videos, blogs, and websites for official organizations.

▼ In 2015, the Canadian government promised to take in at least 25,000 Syrian refugees. Many were greeted at Lester B. Pearson International Airport in Toronto, Ontario by people who were once refugees.

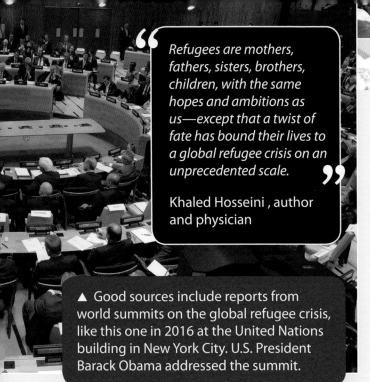

Refugees are mothers, fathers, sisters, brothers, children, with the same hopes and ambitions as us—except that a twist of fate has bound their lives to a global refugee crisis on an unprecedented scale.

Khaled Hosseini , author and physician

▲ Good sources include reports from world summits on the global refugee crisis, like this one in 2016 at the United Nations building in New York City. U.S. President Barack Obama addressed the summit.

COUNTRIES OF ORIGIN OF MOST REFUGEES

Syria	
Afghanistan	
South Sudan	
Myanmar	
Somalia	
Sudan	
Democratic Republic of the Congo	
Central African Republic	

Number of refugees (millions)
0 1 2 3 4 5 6 7

Figures for 2017 from United Nations Refugee Agency

KEEPING IT REAL

While some of the information you find online is created by experts or people with personal experience, much of it is not. Keep in mind that some of the facts you find on the Internet could be fake, misleading, or include extreme opinions.

Good sources of information about all aspects of immigration and refugees include:

- experts who have researched and written studies on migration or who have worked closely with immigrants and refugees
- United Nations' and aid agencies' visuals such as graphs, charts, maps, and diagrams that display facts and statistics in a way that is easier to digest
- interviews with immigrants and refugees by **credible** print, radio, and television reporters and journalists
- reports and statistics from governments about their immigrants and refugees
- websites created by nonprofit groups dedicated to helping immigrants and refugees in their homelands, temporary homes, and host countries
- statements from politicians and esteemed world leaders on **social media** sites, such as Twitter, Instagram, and Facebook.

Sources of information need to be analyzed and interpreted to determine their meaning and significance. There is no single correct way to interpret a source but it can be misinterpreted. People have different opinions and perspectives that influence their viewpoint, and you need to be alert and sensitive to this at all times. Also be aware that some viewpoints and perspectives are not based on facts but on feelings or a desire to persuade people to think a certain way.

Over time, values and ideas shift and change as people learn new facts or details. Concepts that were once generally accepted may no longer be in favor. It is important to allow for any factors that may have influenced the person who created the source.

CRITICAL REVIEW

To ensure you have a balanced view from a variety of perspectives, use many different source materials. Each source should be accurate and credible. To help you interpret a source and determine its value, ask the questions listed on the opposite page. If the answers raise any concerns, discard the source.

▼ A person's own experiences and prior knowledge of a topic help shape the way they interpret a source.

ASK YOUR OWN QUESTIONS

There are six key questions to ask when gathering information about a subject. These questions should also be answered in an article or report in order to help you gain a complete understanding of the topic. They are:

• Who was involved?
• What happened?
• When did it take place?
• Where did it take place?
• Why did it happen?
• How did it happen?

▶ *Escape from Syria* is a graphic novel based on the real-life experiences of refugees who fled from Syria. Written by a migration and conflict journalist, it is a great source.

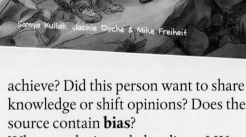

Samya Kullab, Jackie Roche & Mike Freiheit

• Who was the creator? Was this person an expert on the topic or did he or she have firsthand experience of it?
• Where and when was the source material created? Were there any key values, events, ideas, people, or other factors at the time that may have influenced the creator's point of view? How do those values and views differ from those today?
• Why was the source material created, and what was the creator hoping to achieve? Did this person want to share knowledge or shift opinions? Does the source contain **bias**?
• Who was the intended audience? Was the creator trying to shift their opinion or did they share the same ideas and values as the creator?
• Does the creator provide good **evidence** to support the main points?
• How does information in the source material compare to that in other sources from a similar time period?

For thousands of years, people have migrated from one place to another for many different reasons. These migrations have had a huge impact on the ethnic, social, and economic aspects of communities, countries, and continents. The first humans lived in Africa as many as 200,000 years ago. They likely began moving to other parts of the world to find better food supplies or to escape the impact of natural disasters such as volcanoes and monsoons.

◄ The history of the world is a history of migration. These refugees were part of the thousands who fled war and terror in the Middle East for safety in Europe from 2015 to 2018.

▼ Natural disasters are major causes of human migration. Hurricane Maria hit Puerto Rico in 2017. Since that time, over 135,000 people have left the devastated island for the U.S. mainland.

ANCIENT MASS MIGRATIONS

At the end of the last Ice Age about 12,000 years ago, people began to migrate from Asia across what was then a land bridge into the continent now known as North America. They spread across the region, establishing new communities and ways of life. For thousands of years, these were the only humans to inhabit the area.

Mass migrations also took place among such ancient cultures as the Greeks, Romans, Turks, Slavs, and Germanic peoples, as they fought wars, sought refuge, and settled new lands.

FOREVER ON THE MOVE

The reasons and prompts for migration have been constant throughout history. Sometimes, people were forced to move from one place to another due to violent conflicts. Invaders from another region took control of their land, or wars between local groups left them caught in the middle and at risk. At other times, people uprooted themselves in search of a better life. The promise of land, freedom, better education, safer communities, work opportunities, and overall improved quality of life tempted people to leave their homelands and try their luck in foreign lands.

In some cases, people were forcibly removed from their homes and taken to other parts of the world to work as slaves or laborers. On many occasions, people were forced to flee due to natural disasters, such as volcanoes, earthquakes, floods, or droughts, that destroyed their land and left them without food, shelter, and water.

About 500 years ago, European explorers began venturing beyond their borders. When they came upon North America for the first time, they wanted to claim control of the land and populate it with people from their own countries. By the early 1600s, a wave of immigration began that would continue over the next several hundred years.

Many early European immigrants were paid to travel. The governments of Britain, France, and Spain sent **colonists** to build permanent homes. Fighting among these nations for control of territories within North America led to more colonists being sent overseas to settle more of the land. Others were indentured servants— people who promised to work for free for some years in exchange for passage to North America and the necessities of life.

DARING JOURNEY

The journey from Europe to North America was difficult. Migrants traveled for weeks on overcrowded ships through seas that were often turbulent. They had limited food to eat, and many people became sick, died, or were lost at sea. Nonetheless, they came in numbers.

Some Europeans saw the move as an opportunity to expand their wealth. They heard of the rich resources in this new land, such as furs, forests, and fish, and hoped to make money trading these goods. Others left Europe in order to escape debtor's prison. If people could not pay their debts for any reason, they were sent to prison until they could. Some immigrants, such as the Pilgrims, wanted to escape religious persecution and practice their own beliefs freely.

▶ From 1500 to the mid-1800s, about 12 million Africans were forcibly taken to the Americas and enslaved as part of the largest forced migration in history. About 500,000 were sent to North America. The rest were sent to South America and the Caribbean.

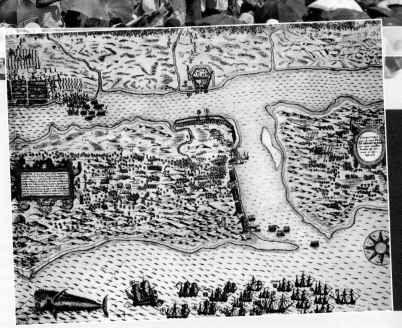

◀ Sir Francis Drake was an explorer who claimed land in America on behalf of England. In 1586, he was sent to attack Spanish settlements such as the stronghold at St. Augustine in Florida, as shown on this map. Historically, Florida had strong links to early British and Spanish immigrants.

Upon their arrival in North America, settlers encountered Indigenous peoples living off the land. While some formed trade relationships with the Indigenous peoples, many others treated them poorly. They forced them off their land and tried to convert them to European ways of life. Many Indigenous peoples were killed in battles or died of European diseases.

> *Remember, remember always, that all of us, and you and I especially, are descended from immigrants and revolutionists.*
>
> Franklin D. Roosevelt, 32nd U.S. president

▼ Today, people migrate to North America for similar reasons as the early European immigrants. At this U.S. Citizenship and Immigration Services' ceremony, 63 people from 22 different countries received their citizenship.

Until the mid-1800s, the majority of North American settlers had come from the British Isles. They were a mix of wealthy **social elite** and laborers who saw North America as a land of opportunity and freedom. Almost all of them were immigrants. However, as the idea that North America offered freedom and opportunity spread, more settlers began to emigrate from Europe. As a result, the largest mass migration in modern history— known as the Great Atlantic Migration—began in the 1840s.

During this period there were few government restrictions on who could enter the United States and Canada. Approximately 50 million people migrated from Europe to the Americas, with more than two-thirds settling in the United States. At first, the majority of migrants

ASK YOUR OWN QUESTIONS

How do you think people already living in North America felt about millions of immigrants arriving? What benefits may they have brought? What areas of conflict may have arisen? Would those issues be similar for immigrants and refugees today?

▼ Irish migrants onboard a ship to America during the Great Irish Famine. In Ireland in the 1840s and 1850s, mass potato crop failures left many people with little to eat. More than one million died and another million or more immigrated to North America.

▲ In 1862, the United States passed the Homestead Act, which gave free land to people who would set up and run farms for a minimum of five years. This is the first homestead claimed, in Gage County, Nebraska.

▶ A railway company poster of 1870 offering free homesteads.

came from Britain, Ireland, France, Scandinavia, Germany, and other parts of northern and western Europe. Separately, from 1848 to 1851, more than 300,000 people, including about 25,000 Chinese—mostly men— immigrated to California as part of the gold rush in that state.

PROMISE OF A BETTER LIFE

From the mid-1800s, factors that influenced Europeans to migrate to North America included famines—for example, in Germany and Ireland (see opposite); political unrest—in France, Russia, and Poland; and better work and business opportunities—for people from Great Britain and Scandinavia.

In North America, the boom in industry led to a growing need for people to work in factories. This boosted both immigration and migration within the continent as people moved from rural areas to industrial towns and cities. The American Civil War (1861–1865) caused immigration to slow, but in 1862 the U.S. government passed the Homestead Act (see above), which opened up the western part of the country to settlement.

◀ From 1916 to 1970, more than six million African Americans in the United States migrated to cities in the North, Midwest, and West in order to overcome poor economic opportunities and harsh **segregationist** laws in the rural South. This period is known as the Great Migration.

"…give me your tired, your poor, your huddled masses yearning to breathe free, the wretched refuse of your teeming shore…."

This poem is written on a plaque on the Statue of Liberty's pedestal. The statue originally represented the end of slavery. Over time, it became a symbol of the nation's immigrant history. It refers to the concept of the American Dream of great opportunities for all.

KEY PLAYERS

Clifford Sifton's immigration policy favored farmers from the United States, people from Scotland and northern England, and peasants from eastern and central Europe. He discouraged shopkeepers, artists, and laborers from moving to Canada. He believed they would want to live in the major cities rather than become pioneers in the West. He thought this would increase the unemployment rate in those places, which were already well populated. Instead, Sifton urged people who were willing to work the land to migrate to Canada.

◄ On January 1, 1892, the U.S. government opened an immigration station on Ellis Island in New York City. Immigrants arriving by ship traded a piece of paper with an entry number for a visa that allowed them entry into the country. Ellis Island processed more than 12 million immigrants between 1892 and 1924. There were other ports of entry, but Ellis Island was the largest.

By the late 1800s, the flow of immigrants from western and northern Europe began to subside. But many immigrants still came, now from countries in southern, central, and eastern Europe such as Italy, Spain, Portugal, Austria-Hungary, and Russia. It was a time of rapid **industrialization** in America, and they saw an opportunity to find work.

In Canada, the federal government encouraged immigration to help populate the western part of the country with European settlers. It offered free homesteads to migrants who fit a certain profile that the nation deemed desirable. Canadian Minister of the Interior Clifford Sifton created an immigration **policy** that led to a large increase in migrants to Canada between 1896 and 1905.

ANTI-IMMIGRANT FEELINGS

In the United States, many people were grateful for the boost immigrants provided to the labor force. However, in some places, mass migration led to anti-immigrant feelings among people who had been born in the country or had lived there a long time. They viewed the newcomers as competition for jobs and, in some cases, discriminated against them for their culture or beliefs.

The American Party was an anti-Catholic **xenophobic** political party that gained popularity among many Protestants in the 1850s. It aimed to prevent people born outside of the United States from voting or running for public office. It also sought to bring in restrictions on immigration and to require people to live in the country for at least 21 years before they could become U.S. citizens. The Chinese Exclusion Act of 1882 prevented more Chinese from immigrating to America on penalty of imprisonment or deportation.

DISPLACED BY WAR

From the 1800s until the start of World War I in 1914, about one million immigrants arrived in the United States each year. There were few restrictions on entry into the country. That all changed when the war started.

During the war, movement beyond European borders was limited. People were encouraged to join their armed forces. Those who could not fight had to take up vacated jobs or work in factories building weapons for the war. Travel by ship across the Atlantic Ocean was dangerous as the conflict spread to the sea and enemy submarines lurked beneath the water. Also, many of the ships that were once used to transport migrants across the Atlantic were converted for military use.

Near the end of World War I in 1918, immigration quotas were created that limited the number of people who could enter the country.

KEY TOPIC

Adolf Hitler was the leader of the Nazi Party and head of the government of Germany from 1933 until his death in 1945. He was responsible for starting World War II (1939–1945) and the Holocaust.

The **Holocaust** was the German **state-sponsored** persecution and genocide of more than six million Jews by the Nazis. Many Roma and Polish people were treated similarly and killed.

Genocide refers to violent acts intended to destroy a group of people based on their race, ethnicity, religion, or nationality.

Concentration camps are places where political prisoners and minority groups are held prisoner and are often punished or killed.

▼ World War I European migrants gather at a station in Paris, France, searching for a new homeland. As they tried to escape hardships in Europe, immigration to North America at that time more or less came to a standstill.

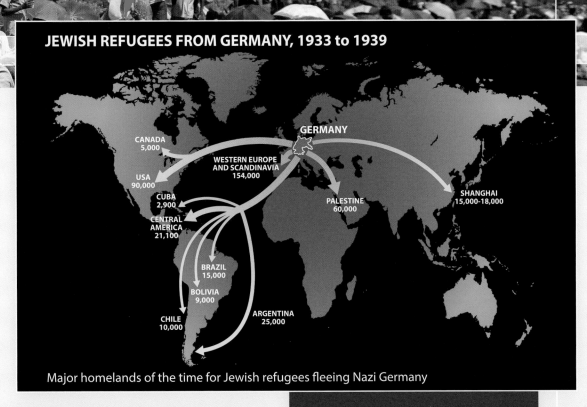

JEWISH REFUGEES FROM GERMANY, 1933 to 1939

GERMANY

CANADA
5,000

WESTERN EUROPE
AND SCANDINAVIA
154,000

USA
90,000

CUBA
2,900

CENTRAL
AMERICA
21,100

PALESTINE
60,000

SHANGHAI
15,000-18,000

BRAZIL
15,000

BOLIVIA
9,000

CHILE
10,000

ARGENTINA
25,000

Major homelands of the time for Jewish refugees fleeing Nazi Germany

Those within the quota had to be able to read and write in their native language. They also had to pass a pre-inspection medical examination before departing from their countries of origin. Canada had similar immigration practices.

▲ Between 1933 and 1940, many Jewish refugees fled Germany to other parts of the world to avoid persecution. This map shows the main regions they were able to settle in and in what numbers.

JEWISH REFUGEES

In 1933, the National Socialist German Workers', or Nazi, Party rose to power in Germany under the leadership of Adolf Hitler. The Nazis believed in the superiority of white Germans. They passed racist laws that discriminated against Jews, Roma people and others. This created a climate of hate that lead to the genocide, or mass murder, of millions in concentration camps. Thousands of Jews looked for refuge in other parts of the world. Like many countries, the United States and Canada were reluctant to take them in. Both were concerned the refugees would be a burden on their economies. They also held racist views that Jews were different and would not mix well with North American society. The two countries also made it difficult for refugees to enter by insisting they have jobs to go to or enough money to support themselves. At that time in North America jobs were hard to find, and most Jews did not have money and possessions with them—the Nazis had stolen them. Yet by 1946, more than 200,000 Jewish refugees gained entry.

Following the two world wars, people began moving from war-torn countries to other parts of the world. Once Europe became more stable, few of its people emigrated. In the 1960s, millions migrated from developing countries to developed, heavily industralized countries.

In the United States, changes to the Immigration Act in 1965 removed quotas to allow more immigrants in.

> " *If DACA denies me, I'm at risk of being deported to one of the most unstable countries in the world, unless I can find a way to leave and make a life elsewhere.* "
>
> Liliana Morales
> (a DREAMer—see below)

However, many Eastern Europeans could not afford to make the move or were not allowed to leave their countries due to new **communist** policies implemented by their governments. With fewer Europeans migrating overseas, there were more opportunities for people from Asia, Africa, the Caribbean, and other parts of the world, and they began to relocate to North America.

While many people chose to immigrate to new countries, refugee crises around the world also forced many to make the move. World leaders called for better policies to support refugees in their times of need. The treatment of Jewish refugees during World War II sparked international **debates** about how to prevent similar **atrocities** in the future.

▶ In 2012, the U.S. government under President Barack Obama created an immigration policy called the Deferred Action for Childhood Arrivals (DACA). It allowed many thousands of people who were brought into the country illegally as children to receive a renewable two-year period of stay so they could live, study, and work in the United States. These children were known as DREAMers.

ASK YOUR OWN QUESTIONS

Imagine you live in a country where life for ordinary people is difficult. What may prompt you to flee to a land you know little about? What would you expect to have to do to settle there?

◀ In January 2017, President Trump signed a **controversial** executive order that temporarily stopped people from **Muslim** countries from gaining entry into the United States. In addition, Trump is attempting to build a wall along the Mexico border to keep illegal immigrants from entering the United States.

CONSIDERING HUMAN RIGHTS

In response, the United Nations created the Universal Declaration of Human Rights in 1948. This document defined the basic rights and freedoms of all people, regardless of their culture, origin, or beliefs. In 1951, it was amended to clarify the difference between immigrants and refugees. It also outlined the right for refugees to seek international protection and entry into another country in the event they were forced to flee their homelands.

Today, globally, one in every 30 people is a migrant. Canada and the United States have long histories as settler nations, which remain to this day. They continue to provide opportunities for migrants to seek better lives within their borders either in the form of **resettlement** or as a temporary stop on their way elsewhere.

Information is easy to find, but it is often unfiltered. From podcasts about the Syrian refugee crisis to brochures from special interest groups about the support they provide to new migrants, it is important to know how to assess content. Each source needs to be analyzed and interpreted to decipher its meaning and **validity**.

Cristina Jiménez is the Executive Director and co-founder of United We Dream (UWD), the largest immigrant youth-led community in the United States. She fled Ecuador with her parents when she was 13 years old. Cristina grew up as an undocumented immigrant in Queens, New York City. She experienced poverty and discrimination and constantly feared deportation. As a DREAMer (see page 24), she decided to stand up for the rights of undocumented immigrants. She was a key player in the **campaign** that led to the creation of DACA.

◄ In 2018, people gathered at the White House in Washington, D.C. to protest President Trump's plan to decrease the number of refugees allowed to enter the country from 45,000 in 2018 to 30,000 in 2019.

DEVELOPING YOUR SKILLS

Information literacy skills are necessary to become an informed citizen and a lifelong learner. They allow you to effectively and efficiently discover, **evaluate**, use, and share information. Having strong information literacy skills makes it easier to sort through the abundance of information to find top-quality materials.

To develop your information literacy skills about immigration and refugees:

- Identify the types and amount of information you need. Then, think about a few key questions you want to answer. Make sure they are clear, measurable, and concise such as, "How many immigrants and refugees come to the United States each year?"
- Find suitable source materials that can help answer your questions, such as government surveys and census reports with facts and figures about the nation's population and countries of origin.
- Evaluate each source with a critical eye to ensure it is credible, reliable, and relevant. Be sure to look for a variety of sources with a range of perspectives. Allow for bias in your research and assessment.
- Consider how deeply you need to research the subject. Too little information and you will not get a balanced view. Too much information and you may not be able to process it thoroughly.
- Share your new knowledge with others. You might create a podcast, report, or blog about why people migrate.

Immigrants are people who choose to leave their homeland to settle in another country. In most cases, they want to become citizens of their new country and to live and work there permanently. They often choose their destination and plan for their departure well in advance. Many will study the culture of their new country and learn its language before they leave. They may take their belongings with them when they depart. Immigrants usually have the freedom to visit and return to their homeland if they wish.

DIFFERENT TYPES OF IMMIGRANTS

Legal immigrants are people who have the proper documentation and meet the legal requirements for entry into their new country and for settlement on a permanent basis. In North America, this may mean they are a member of the family of a U.S. or

THE CENTRAL ISSUES

About 86 percent of refugees seek safety in developing nations. These nations often do not have the financial stability to support them. What can other people around the world do to help make sure refugees in these places have access to food, shelter, fresh water, and health care?

▼ In 2018, President Trump announced that DACA would no longer be accepted and DREAMers would lose their status by March 2020.

IN LIFE

Bill Nye hopes to save the world on new Netflix series

KARLIE KLOSS AND BILL NYE BY EDDY CHEN, NETFLIX

USA TODAY™ WEEKEND

DREAMers lose protections

Deportations up under Trump administration

"This is more evidence that the Trump administration is making nearly every person who's undocumented a priority for removal." Ali Noorani, National Immigration Forum

Alan Gomez
@alangomez
USA TODAY

The Trump administration has stepped up the deportation of undocumented immigrants who came to the USA as children and lost their protected status, which had allowed them to stay, according to federal data provided to USA TODAY.

Both the Obama and Trump administrations revoked the Deferred Action for Childhood Arrivals (DACA) status of enrollees who committed serious crimes, affiliated with gangs or were threats to public safety. Under Obama, that led to 365 former DACA enrollees being deported, an average of seven a month since the first DACA applications were approved in September 2012.

In the first month of Donald Trump's presidency, 43 former DACA enrollees were deported, according to Department of Homeland Security statistics requested by USA TODAY.

"This is more evidence that the Trump administration is making nearly every person who's undocumented a priority for removal," said Ali Noorani, executive director of the National Immigration Forum, a group that advocates for immigrants in the USA. "That's a really poor use of law enforcement resources."

President Obama created DACA to protect undocumented immigrants brought to the country before they turned 16.

Under the program, those with no significant criminal records who were going to school or graduated could submit an application to the federal government. If approved by the Department of Homeland Security, the immigrants were protected from deportation for two years and could receive a work permit. They could reapply to extend their DACA status for an additional two years. More than 750,000 people were approved for the program, and the vast majority were granted a renewal.

DACA was not an absolute guarantee. If an enrollee was convicted of a felony, a "significant misdemeanor" or three other misdemeanors, his or her protections

FREDERIC J. BROWN, AFP/GETTY IMAGES

Police arrest demonstrators protesting immigration enforcement in Los Angeles.

▶ STORY CONTINUES ON 2A

Canadian resident—a parent, child, husband, or wife, for example. They may also be part of a program to bring workers with much-needed skills into the country. In Canada, for example, business immigrants are people allowed to enter because they own a business, are investors, or entrepreneurs.

Undocumented immigrants do not have the legal right to live and work in a country. Some enter legally at first but then remain after their immigration documents expire. Others find a way to sneak in and bypass the legal process. A number apply to stay in the country while they are visiting but are denied and must leave.

Governments and residents of the new countries have mixed feelings about immigrants. Some people think they help the country grow and **prosper**. Others believe they challenge the existing way of life or heritage of the country. Large numbers of immigrants cause concern.

> There's an understanding in Canada that immigration is a net-positive for our society and that we should continue to have a very robust immigration system that welcomes those in need of protection but also those that want to come and give us their skills and talents.
>
> Ahmed Hussen, Canadian Minister of Immigration, Refugees and Citizenship

Refugees are people who are forced to leave their homeland. They often fear for their lives if they remain where they are. Conflicts in the **Middle East**, gang violence in Southeast Asia, and religious persecution in places such as Pakistan and Myanmar are just a few of the reasons why many people today emigrate in search of a safer place to live.

▶ There has been a sharp increase in the number of illegal immigrants and undocumented refugees crossing Canada's borders in recent years. In the first three months of 2017, the Royal Canadian Mounted Police (RCMP) discovered 1,890 people trying to cross the border illegally. There were 5,052 during the same period in 2018.

NATIONALITY OF PEOPLE ABLE TO SEEK ASYLUM IN THE U.S. IN 2017

All other countries 30%

China 22%

El Salvador 11%

Guatemala 10%

Honduras 7%

Ethiopia

Nepal

Iraq

Syria

Egypt

Mexico

Total number of successful asylum applications in 2017 was 60,566

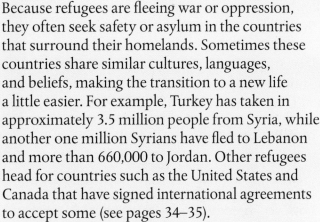

Because refugees are fleeing war or oppression, they often seek safety or asylum in the countries that surround their homelands. Sometimes these countries share similar cultures, languages, and beliefs, making the transition to a new life a little easier. For example, Turkey has taken in approximately 3.5 million people from Syria, while another one million Syrians have fled to Lebanon and more than 660,000 to Jordan. Other refugees head for countries such as the United States and Canada that have signed international agreements to accept some (see pages 34–35).

Refugees often risk their lives to leave their countries. They may pile into overcrowded fishing boats or rafts to travel across dangerous waters. Others make the journey on foot, sometimes through freezing-cold conditions or along trails monitored by violent gangs. Many never reach their destination, dying as a result of the harsh conditions along the way.

RECEIVING A HELPING HAND

Refugees often live in a state of limbo. They do not know if they will gain citizenship in the places to which they flee or if these countries are a temporary stop while they await news of a permanent host. Often, refugees are resettled in places far from their own homelands.

For instance, more than one million Syrians have made their way to Europe since 2011. Germany has taken in about 500,000, making it the fifth-largest displaced Syrian population in the world. Other Syrians have sought safety in even more distant lands. About 54,000 Syrians have resettled in Canada and 33,000 in the United States. There they are given places to stay, food to eat, and help learning the main language and finding jobs.

PUBLIC OPINION

Factors such as national security concerns or public opinion surrounding certain races or cultures play a role in immigration and refugee policies. Some people believe high immigration levels are a major concern. They worry newcomers will compete with them for jobs, overstretch the **infrastructure**, or cost taxpayers too much money. This is because governments sometimes provide support programs to help immigrants and refugees adjust to their new lives. Over time, however, migrants typically pay more in taxes and bring more to society than they take from it.

Other people believe immigrants and refugees are a threat to society. In France, for example, 56 percent of people believe immigration has

▲ In 2018, thousands of migrants lived in illegal camps in Paris, France. Many of them were refugees from Somalia, Sudan, and Eritrea.

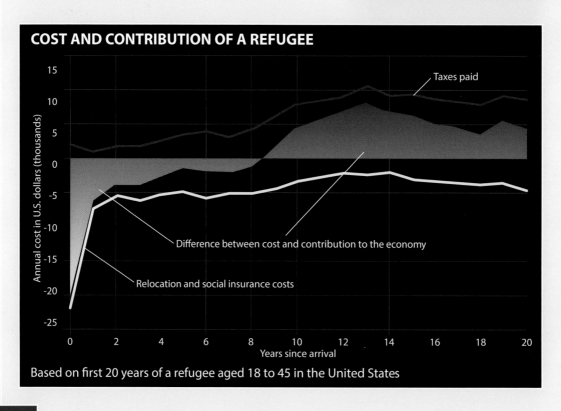

COST AND CONTRIBUTION OF A REFUGEE

Annual cost in U.S. dollars (thousands)

Taxes paid

Difference between cost and contribution to the economy

Relocation and social insurance costs

Years since arrival

Based on first 20 years of a refugee aged 18 to 45 in the United States

◄ In North America, new immigrants and refugees are first attracted to large cities, such as New York City, where they consider opportunities to settle and find work the greatest.

a negative impact on the country. Many people believe the country should close its doors to refugees altogether for the time being. In the United Kingdom, citizens voted to withdraw their country from the European Union in part because they disagreed with the organization's rule allowing the free movement of thousands of migrants between the 28 countries who are members. In the United States, some fear that **Islamophobia** is influencing immigration policies.

OVERCOMING OBSTACLES

Regardless of how or why people leave their homelands, adjusting to life in a new country comes with many challenges. Many migrants do not speak the local language, making it hard to find jobs, make friends, or do schoolwork. For many immigrants and refugees, their culture, the clothes they wear, and the foods they eat may be very different from those of their new home. They may need to adjust their ways of life with those of the people where they now live.

SEARCH TIPS

There are search tools for finding an expert on a topic such as immigrants and refugees. Type the subject into the search bar. This will help you find experts doing up-to-date research.

Google Scholar: https://scholar.google.ca

Microsoft Academic: https://academic. microsoft.com

Expertise Finder: http://expertisefinder.com

Most countries have immigration policies that help regulate the flow of people coming in. In the United States and Canada, immigration policies often center on the need to boost the economy and provide a steady flow of laborers. In Canada, most people believe the policies are good. When asked if immigration levels are too high, 60 percent of Canadians said no and 80 percent believed newcomers contributed positively to the economy.

COMPLEX QUALIFICATIONS

Typically, immigration policies are set up to benefit the host countries, not the migrants. Immigrants are required to meet complex requirements and qualifications before they are allowed to enter those countries. In most cases,

ASK YOUR OWN QUESTIONS

Imagine you are the head of a government department making a policy about allowing refugees into the country. What factors and whose views will you consider? Will you give all refugees an equal chance? If not, why?

▼ In 2018, it was revealed that immigrant and refugee children from Mexico and Central America were being separated from their families at the U.S. border and housed in private shelters. The public outcry and worldwide backlash led to a change in the policy.

they must maintain a certain level of education or have a special skill set that the host's people lack. They must also pass medical examinations and security checks. It usually takes years to fulfill all the immigration needs. In some cases, immigrants may be part of a special program that reunites families or allows entry for highly skilled individuals.

Most countries have separate immigration and refugee policies. They outline the circumstances for accepting refugees within their borders. The United Nations High Commissioner for Refugees (UNHCR) helps determine if a person qualifies as a refugee or asylum seeker under international law. This long, complicated process ensures refugees are documented so they can be considered for settlement or resettlement in a host country. Host countries are ultimately responsible for deciding the status of asylum seekers, but the UNHCR assists in cases where the country does not have the means or is unwilling to do so.

▶ The UNHCR is dedicated to saving lives and protecting the rights of refugees to seek safety in other parts of the world.

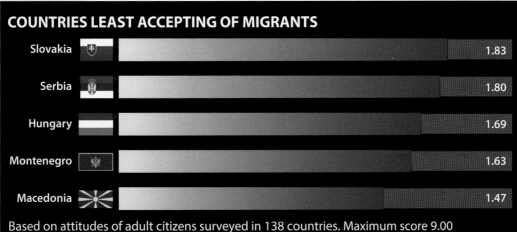

COUNTRIES LEAST ACCEPTING OF MIGRANTS

Country	Score
Slovakia	1.83
Serbia	1.80
Hungary	1.69
Montenegro	1.63
Macedonia	1.47

Based on attitudes of adult citizens surveyed in 138 countries. Maximum score 9.00

5 STAYING INFORMED

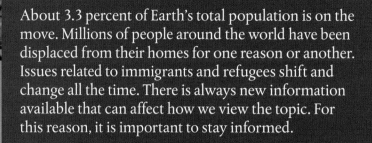

About 3.3 percent of Earth's total population is on the move. Millions of people around the world have been displaced from their homes for one reason or another. Issues related to immigrants and refugees shift and change all the time. There is always new information available that can affect how we view the topic. For this reason, it is important to stay informed.

◄ Some people want their governments to allow fewer people into their countries. They may hold protests, such as this anti-Muslim gathering in Toronto, to campaign for their cause.

THE CENTRAL ISSUES

Conflicts, natural disasters, political unrest, unemployment, and differences in beliefs can and do happen in any country. Do immigrants and refugees always benefit from leaving their homeland for another country? What factors may they consider in deciding they now have a better— or worse—life?

◀ In February 2017, 153 Guatemalan immigrants were sent back to their homeland aboard a deportation flight out of Texas. Border agents catch more illegal immigrants crossing the Mexican border in Texas than in any other state.

CRITICAL REVIEW

Staying informed about any major issue requires a critical assessment of world situations. You need to look beyond local sources of news and information to gain an international perspective and balanced view. As a result, your conclusions may go against that of people within your community or the official view of your nation's government. But providing you have done your research well, they are valid and worthy of being supported and listened to by others.

Some good specific source materials for learning about immigration and refugees include:

- government and international policy and awareness websites such as the Immigration and Refugee Board of Canada, the U.S. Office of Refugee Resettlement, and the UNHCR
- nonprofit groups such as Amnesty International, UNICEF, Young Center for Immigrant Children's Rights, Canadian Council for Refugees, and United We Dream
- documentaries and truth-based movies about real-life stories of immigrants and refugees such as *4.1 Miles*, *Refugee*, and *Which Way Home*. Also watch TV documentaries on the topic from CNN, PBS, and the BBC
- blogs on official sites such as Refugees International, the American Immigration Council, and Refugee Research Network
- children's books such as *Refugee* by Alan Gratz and *Escape from Syria* by Samya Kullab
- experts and activists such as Cristina Jiménez, Mariana Atencio, and Omar C. Jadwat.

The number of people forced to flee their homeland is at its highest rate since World War II. There are more than 25 million refugees and about 40 million internally displaced persons around the world. Approximately 34,000 people a day have no choice but to leave their homes. Experts project there could be more than 405 million international migrants by 2050. Myanmar, South Sudan, Yemen, and Syria are just a few of the countries facing major refugee crises today.

FOREIGN AID

Some countries provide resources, such as food and medical aid, to those parts of the world to which refugees are fleeing. They may also fund nonprofit organizations that provide other on-the-ground assistance during a crisis. Others provide aid only to the countries from which they receive the most refugees. A country's reasons for giving, or not giving, foreign aid are many and varied, and they change quickly.

WORKING TOGETHER

Nonprofit organizations often work with refugees to ensure they are treated fairly and humanely. Many, such as Amnesty International, the Red Cross, and Refugees International, provide resources within the countries where people are in need. In these places, people often lack food, health care facilities, education, and shelter.

Many migrants and displaced people do not qualify as refugees and have no other place to go. This is true of people fleeing the destruction of natural disasters. Nonprofit organizations provide care for these people and also offer services to migrants once they are resettled in their temporary or permanent homes.

> *All of these emerging trends pose enormous challenges for the international humanitarian community. The threat of continued massive displacement is real, and the world must be prepared to deal with it.*
>
> United Nations

ASK YOUR OWN QUESTIONS

More people are migrating today than any other time in history. Why do you think this is? What events take place today that may cause people to leave their homes? Why would they travel to developing, not developed, countries?

▶ A refugee camp in Bangladesh that houses the Rohingya people from the country of Myanmar. The Rohingya are a Muslim minority who have been persecuted in their home country for many years. They have migrated to neighboring countries to flee deadly attacks.

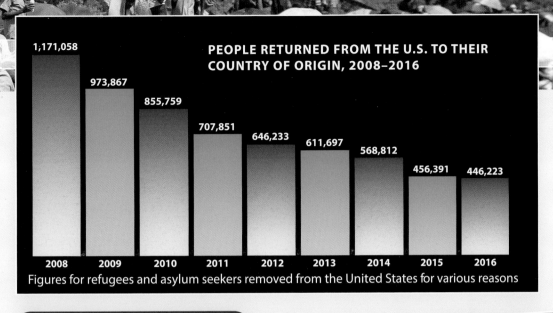

PEOPLE RETURNED FROM THE U.S. TO THEIR COUNTRY OF ORIGIN, 2008–2016

- 2008: 1,171,058
- 2009: 973,867
- 2010: 855,759
- 2011: 707,851
- 2012: 646,233
- 2013: 611,697
- 2014: 568,812
- 2015: 456,391
- 2016: 446,223

Figures for refugees and asylum seekers removed from the United States for various reasons

▶ In October 2017, these Rohingya refugees were held at the border of Bangladesh, where they wanted to migrate until conditions were safe for them to return to Myanmar.

6 KEEPING UP TO DATE

To stay informed about a topic, you need to continue to monitor the issue and any new developments. This is particularly true for immigrants and refugees as world politics, economics, and international relationships change on an almost daily basis.

▶ Greece has been deeply impacted by refugee crises. About 11,000 refugees and migrants arrived in the country in 2018 compared to about 2,500 in 2017, putting a strain on the nation's services. In October 2018, Iranian refugees protested in Athens. They were seeking better rights, a faster asylum process, and accommodation since many do not have a place to stay.

SEARCH TIPS

When looking at websites, address extensions can help pinpoint what sort of information you may be getting.

.gov (government)—restricted to use by government entities.

.org (organization)—anyone can register for this, although it is often used for nonprofit organizations and charities.

.com (commercial)—originally for businesses, it is the most widely used extension.

Country extensions:
.ca Canada
.au Australia
.uk United Kingdom
.ru Russia
.de Germany

YOUR OWN NEWS DIET

The Internet provides a constant stream of information from across the globe, and you can get information from it whenever it is convenient for you. But don't make it your only source. Not all information is created equally. Even the media crafts messages in a way that can influence people's behaviors and beliefs.

One of the best ways to keep up to date on current affairs is to create a **news diet**. It includes a variety of sources of information to ensure you get a well-balanced view of the issue. Use these sources and guidelines to stay informed:

- Read major newspapers and magazines, such as *Time*, *The New York Times*, *The Wall Street Journal*, and *USA Today*, and check out *The Refugee Brief*.
- Talk with friends, family, and teachers about current affairs. Be open to new perspectives.
- Set up a Google alert for news stories about immigration and global refugee crises, so you always have the latest information.
- Tune into radio interviews, panels, and discussions with aid workers, world leaders, and governments about migration topics.
- Stream fact-based news media on the Internet such as CNN's *Immigration News*, and National Public Radio's (NPR) *Stories about Immigration*.
- Listen to podcasts by immigrants and refugees about their personal experiences.
- Volunteer to work with groups that help immigrants and refugees.
- Meet with people who do not share your own point of view on the topic to discuss their views.

WHAT YOU CAN DO

Some people are fortunate to be born in communities where they are free to practice their beliefs, have access to education and jobs, and do not fear violence or conflict. Many others are born into turmoil and denied their basic rights. Everyone deserves to be treated fairly and humanely.

IMPACT ON SOCIETY

Immigrants and refugees entering a country enrich local culture and perspectives on global issues. They contribute to the economy by paying taxes, bringing skills and resources to workplaces, and increasing the demand for the products and services they consume. However, large numbers of migrants can place great stress on the host country's infrastructure. It is important to research and understand all perspectives in order to form your own opinion on the topic.

RAISING AWARENESS, GIVING HELP

There are steps you can take to help immigrants and refugees get the support they need both in their homelands and in their host countries. Building awareness of global issues and how they impact the people in other parts of the world is one way. Another is to research world issues and then share what you learn with friends and family so they can better understand why immigrants and refugees migrate to new places.

You can also write to politicians to ask them to take action by providing aid to countries in need and assistance to newcomers. You can even volunteer to work with local groups that help migrants settle in your community or with international organizations providing aid, or you can donate money to a refugee support group.

LOW RISK **HIGH RISK**

WHAT'S AT STAKE?
Think about your own community. Are there any immigrants or refugees living there? What reasons did they have to come to your community? What can you do to help them feel supported and welcome?

▶ Studying in groups is a great way to enhance your learning. Group members can share their unique perspectives and learn from one another.

42

▲ In June 2018, construction began on a 14-mile-long (22.5 km) wall along the border between San Diego, California, and Tijuana, Mexico. Construction on similar walls started in Calexico, California, and Santa Teresa, New Mexico, earlier that year. They are part of President Trump's initiative to better secure the U.S. border.

SEARCH TIPS

Use quotation marks around a phrase to search for that exact combination of words (for example, "refugee camp").

Use a colon and an extension to search a specific site (for example, Refugee:.gov for all government website mentions of the topic).

Use the word Define and a colon to search for word definitions (for example, Define: infrastructure).

GLOSSARY

analyzing Studying in detail, thoroughly

atrocities Actions that are extremely cruel

bias Favoring one view over another

campaign A plan with a specific purpose

civil war Conflict between people within a country

colonists People living in colonies, which are areas of a country ruled by another country

communist A person or government that supports the idea of a society in which all property and wealth is shared and available as needed

complacent Feeling secure or content with a situation because one is not aware of potential dangers

conflict A major disagreement between opposing parties

controversial Causing disagreement over a certain matter

credible Able to be trusted or believed

debates Discussion where all sides and perspectives of a topic are considered

deported Sent back to one's homeland

detained Held against one's wishes

discrimination Act of treating someone with less favor than someone else

emigrated Left one country to resettle in another

evaluate Judge or determine the value of something

evidence Facts or information that prove if something is true or real

host countries Countries that take in an immigrant or refugee

Indigenous peoples Original inhabitants of a region or country; sometimes called First Nations, Aboriginal, or Native people

industrialization The wide-scale development of industries

infrastructure Systems of a city or country such as the transportation and health care networks

interpreting Explaining the meanings of something

Islamophobia Fear and prejudice against Islam and Muslims

media Methods of mass communication such as TV and radio

Middle East A region in western Asia and northern Africa

Muslim A person who follows Islam

natural disasters Extreme and often sudden events

news diet The sources used to get news

persecution The ill-treatment of people because of their race, culture, or beliefs

policy An idea or plan used to guide decision-making

prosper To do well or become successful

resettlement The act of settling in a different place

segregationist Favoring separating people by race

social elite People who belong to the upper class or believe they are superior to others

social media Websites and computer software that let people communicate and share opinions

society People who live together within a certain community

source materials Collections of information and evidence on a topic

state-sponsored Paid for by the government

statistics A type of math that deals with the analysis and presentation of numerical data

tolerance To treat others fairly whatever their race, culture, and beliefs

validity The state of being factual and accurate

visa A permit to enter and stay in a country for a time

xenophobic Fear, hatred, or prejudice toward people from other countries

SOURCE NOTES

QUOTATIONS

p. 5 https://www.nytimes.com/2017/01/28/world/canada/justin-trudeau-trump-refugee-ban.html

p. 6 https://www.thereportertimes.com/others/world-refugee-day-2017-quotes-theme-date-history/

p. 11 https://www.globalgiving.org/learn/listicle/12-shareable-world-refugee-day-quotes/

p. 17 https://cssh.northeastern.edu/policyschool/2017/05/immigrants-and-revolutionists/

p. 20 https://www.loc.gov/item/2016685948/

p. 24 http://www.latimes.com/projects/la-na-daca-recipients/

p. 29 https://www.businessinsider.com/canada-minister-immigration-america-2017-4

p. 38 https://www.care.org/emergencies/global-refugee-crisis

REFERENCES USED FOR THIS BOOK

Chapter 1: People on the Move, pp. 4–7
https://tinyurl.com/ybmr99wp
https://tinyurl.com/yah8hdnr
https://tinyurl.com/hv6fxw6
https://tinyurl.com/yco6qvf9
https://tinyurl.com/y9lussal
https://tinyurl.com/ybtsgkns

Chapter 2: How to Get Informed, pp. 8–13
https://tinyurl.com/ltdobnp
https://tinyurl.com/ybbzjut5
https://tinyurl.com/y979xkz

Chapter 3: The Big Picture, pp. 14–25
https://tinyurl.com/yd45n3bg
https://tinyurl.com/hygsprt
https://tinyurl.com/ne2na8p
https://tinyurl.com/yck6s3mx
https://tinyurl.com/y8oplnpt
https://tinyurl.com/y77m7ho7
https://tinyurl.com/ydhr3qgl
https://tinyurl.com/yafq7zc3
https://tinyurl.com/yawn4wf7
https://tinyurl.com/yc2sqh24
https://tinyurl.com/plddr3k
https://tinyurl.com/hfj9o5m

Chapter 4: An Informed Decision, pp. 26–35
https://tinyurl.com/ya8qtl6n
https://tinyurl.com/y96umlr8
https://tinyurl.com/y9ccd445
https://tinyurl.com/yben8yug
https://tinyurl.com/ybf8jpol
https://tinyurl.com/y7rxogqn
https://tinyurl.com/ybe5nrsf

Chapter 5: Staying Informed, pp. 36–39
https://tinyurl.com/y75ew2la
https://tinyurl.com/y86je2cu
https://tinyurl.com/y9y2uafs
https://tinyurl.com/y75ew2la
https://tinyurl.com/yacy3m47

Chapter 6: Keeping up to Date, pp. 40–43
https://tinyurl.com/y8znh6f4
https://tinyurl.com/yb4cm3rk
https://tinyurl.com/ybqafs2v

FIND OUT MORE

Finding good source material on the Internet can sometimes be a challenge. When analyzing how reliable the information is, consider these points:

- Who is the author of the page? Is it an expert in the field or a person who experienced the event?

- Is the site well known and up to date? A page that has not been updated for several years probably has out-of-date information.

- Can you verify the facts with another site? Always double-check information.

- Have you checked all possible sites? Don't just look on the first page a search engine provides.

- Remember to try government sites and research papers.

- Have you recorded website addresses and names? Keep this data so you can backtrack later and verify the information you want to use.

WEBSITES
United Nations Universal Declaration of Human Rights for Children and Youth
https://libraryresources.unog.ch/ UDHRforchildren/home

Caring for Kids, a guide for health professionals working with migrant children
https://www.kidsnewtocanada.ca/

United We Dream
https://unitedwedream.org/

Against All Odds, an educational game from the UN that allows you to experience what it is like to be a refugee
http://www.playagainstallodds.ca/ game_us.html

BOOKS
Cunningham, Anne C. *Critical Perspectives on Immigrants and Refugees.* Enslow Publishing, 2016.

Flatt, Lizann. *Immigration.* Crabtree Publishing, 2015.

Kullab, Samya, Jackie Roche, and Mike Freiheit. *Escape from Syria.* Firefly Books, 2017.

Nazario, Sonia. *Enrique's Journey.* Ember Publishing, 2014.

Thorpe, Helen. *The Newcomers: Finding Refuge, Friendship, and Hope in America.* Scribner, 2017.

ABOUT THE AUTHOR
Heather C. Hudak has written hundreds of books for children. When she's not writing, Heather loves traveling and has been to more than 50 countries.

INDEX